*Essential Poems*

**Charlotte Mew**

Copyright © this edition Hannah Wilson

First Edition, 2013

ISBN: 978-1492350477

The author has asserted their moral right under the Copyright, Designs and Patents Act, 1988, to be identified as the author of this work.

All Rights reserved. No part of this publication may be reproduced, copied, stored in a retrieval system, or transmitted, in any form or by any means, without the prior written consent of the copyright holder, nor be otherwise circulated in any form of binding or cover other than that in which it is published and without a similar condition being imposed on the subsequent purchaser. This is a work of fiction: any resemblance to persons living or dead is purely coincidental.

# CONTENTS

| | |
|---|---|
| The Farmer's Bride | 7 |
| Fame | 9 |
| The Narrow Door | 11 |
| The Fête | 12 |
| Beside the Bed | 19 |
| In Nunhead Cemetery | 20 |
| The Peddler | 24 |
| Pècheresse | 25 |
| The Changeling | 27 |
| Ken | 29 |
| A Quoi Bon Dire | 31 |
| The Quiet House | 33 |
| On the Asylum Road | 36 |
| Jour des Morts | 37 |
| The Forest Road | 37 |
| Madeleine in Church | 40 |
| Exspecto Resurrectionam | 51 |
| On the Road to the Sea | 52 |
| The Sunlit House | 54 |

| | |
|---|---|
| The Shade-Catchers | 55 |
| Le Sacré Coeur | 56 |
| Song | 57 |
| Saturday Market | 58 |
| Arracombe Wood | 60 |
| Sea Love | 61 |
| The Road to Kerity | 61 |
| I Have Been through the Gates | 62 |
| The Cenotaph | 63 |
| In the Fields | 64 |
| From a Window | 64 |
| Not for That City | 65 |
| Rooms | 65 |
| Monsieur Qui Passe | 66 |
| Fin de Fête | 67 |
| I So Liked Spring | 68 |
| May 1915 | 69 |
| Old Shepherd's Prayer | 69 |
| On Youth Struck Down | 70 |

| | |
|---|---|
| My Heart is Lame | 70 |
| The Call | 71 |
| Absence | 72 |
| The Trees are Down | 73 |
| Smile, Death | 75 |
| To a Child in Death | 76 |
| Moorland Night | 77 |
| At the Convent Gate | 78 |
| Requiescat | 79 |
| The Little Portress | 81 |
| Afternoon Tea | 83 |
| Song | 84 |
| An Ending | 85 |
| Left Behind | 87 |
| A Farewell | 87 |
| To a Little Child in Death | 88 |
| The Voice | 90 |

# The Farmer's Bride

Three summers since I chose a maid,
Too young maybe-but more's to do
At harvest-time that a bide and woo.
    When us was wed she turned afraid
Of love and me and all things human;
Like the shut of winter's day
Her smile went out, and `twadn't a woman-
    More like a little frightened fay.
        One night, in the Fall, she runned away.

"Out 'mong the sheep, her be," they said,
Should properly have been abed;
But sure enough she wadn't there
Lying awake with her wide brown stare.
So over seven-acre field and up-along across the down
    We chased her, flying like a hare
    Before out lanterns. To Church-Town
        All in a shiver and a scare
We caught her, fetched her home at last
    And turned the key upon her, fast.

    She does the work about the house
    As well as most, but like a mouse:
        Happy enough to cheat and play
        With birds and rabbits and such as they,

So long as men-folk keep away
"Not near, not near!" her eyes beseech
When one of us comes within reach.
      The woman say that beasts in stall
      Look round like children at her call.
      *I've* hardly heard her speak at all.
Shy as a leveret, swift as he,
Straight and slight as a young larch tree,
Sweet as the first wild violets, she,
To her wild self. But what to me?

The short days shorten and the oaks are brown,
      The blue smoke rises to the low grey sky,
One leaf in the still air falls slowly down,
      A magpie's spotted feathers lie
An the black earth spread white with rime,
The berries redden up to Christmas-time.
      What's Christmas-time without there be
      Some other in the house than we!

      She sleeps up in the attic there
      Alone, poor maid. 'Tis but a stair
Betwixt us. Oh! my God! the down,
The soft young down of her, the brown,
The brown of her-her eyes, her hair, her hair!

# Fame

Sometimes in the over-heated house, but not for long,

    Smirking and speaking rather loud,

  I see myself among the crowd,

Where no one fits the singer to his song,

Or sifts the unpainted from the painted faces

Of the people who are always on my stair;

They were not with me when I walked in heavenly places;

    But could I spare

In the blind Earth's great silences and spaces,

  The din, the scuffle, the long stare

  If I went back and it was not there?

Back to the old known things that are the new,

The folded glory of the gorse, the sweetbriar air,

To the larks that cannot praise us, knowing nothing of what we do,

    And the divine, wise trees that do not care.

Yet, to leave Fame, still with such eyes and that bright hair!

God! If I might! And before I go hence

    Take in her stead

    To our tossed bed

One little dream, no matter how small, how wild.

Just now, I think I found it in a field, under a fence -

A frail, dead, new-born lamb, ghostly and pitiful and white

    A blot upon the night,

    The moon's dropped child!

# The Narrow Door

    The narrow door, the narrow door
      On the three steps of which the cafe children play
      Mostly at shop with pebbles from the shore,
    It is always shut this narrow door
But open for a little while to-day.

And round it, each with pebbles in his hand,
A silenced crowd the cafe children stand
To see the long box jerking down the bend
Of twisted stair ; then set on end,
Quite filling up the narrow door
Till it comes out and does not go in any more.

    Along the quay you see it wind.
The slow black line. Someone pulls up the blind
Of the small window just above the narrow door —
    "Tiens ! que veux-tu acheter?" Renee cries,
    "Mais, pour quat'sous, des oignons," Jean replies
And one pays down with pebbles from the shore.

# The Fête

    To-night again the moon's white mat
    Stretches across the dormitory floor
While outside, like an evil cat
    The *pion* prowls down the dark corridor,
    Planning, I know, to pounce on me, in spite
For getting leave to sleep in town last night.
But it was none of us who made that noise,
    Only the old brown owl that hoots and flies
Out of the ivy - he will say it was us boys -
    *Seigneur mon Dieu*: the *sacré* soul of spies!
    He would like to catch each dream that lies
        Hidden behind our sleepy eyes:
Their dream ? But mine-it is the moon and the wood that sees;
All my long life how I shall hate the trees!

In the *Place d'Armes* the dusty planes, all Summer through,
Dozed with the market women in the sun and scarcely stirred
    To see the quiet things that crossed the Square -,
A tiny funeral, the flying shadow of a bird,
    The hump-backed barber Celéstin Lemaire,
      Old Madame Michel in her three-wheeled chair,
        And filing past to Vespers, two and two,
          The *demoiselles* of the *pensionnat*
Towed like a ship through the harbour bar,

Safe into port, where *le petit Jésus*
Perhaps makes nothing of the look they shot at you:
*Si, c'est defendu, mais que voulez-vous?*
It was the sun. The sunshine weaves
A pattern on dull stones: the sunshine leaves
    The portraiture of dreams upon the eyes
        Before it dies:
    All Summer through
The dust hung white upon the drowsy planes
Till suddenly they woke with the Autumn rains.


    It is not only the little boys
        Who have hardly got away from toys,
But I, who am seventeen next year,
Some nights, in bed, have grown cold to hear
    That lonely passion of the rain
Which makes you think of being dead,
And of somewhere living to lay your head
    As if you were a child again,
Crying for one thing, known and near
Your empty heart, to still the hunger and the fear
    That pelts and beats with it against the pane.


    But I remember smiling too
At all the sun's soft tricks and those Autumn dreads
    In winter time, when the grey light broke slowly through

The frosted window-lace to drag us shivering from our beds.

    And when at dusk the singing wind swung down

Straight from the stars to the dark country roads

        Beyond the twinkling town,

    Striking the leafless poplar boughs as he went by,

Like some poor, stray dog by the wayside lying dead,

We left behind us the old world of dread,

I and the wind as we strode whistling on under the Winter sky.


And then in Spring for three days came the Fair

    Just as the planes were starting into bud

Above the caravans: you saw the dancing bear

    Pass on his chain; and heard the jingle and the thud.

        Only four days ago

        They let you out of this dull show

To slither down the *montagne russe* and chaff the man à la tête de veau

        Hit, slick, the bull's eye at the *tir*,

Spin round and round till your head went queer

On the *porcs-roulants*. Oh! là là! *fête!*

*Va pour du vin, et le tête-a-tête*

With the girl who sugars the gaufres! Pauvrette,

    How thin she was! but she smiled, you bet,

    As she took your tip -"One does not forget

The good days, Monsieur". Said with a grace,

But *sacrebleu!* what a ghost of a face!

    And no fun too for the *demoiselles*

Of the *pensionnat*, who were hurried past,

    With their *"Oh, que c'est beau - Ah, qu'elle est belle!"*

A lap-dog's life from first to last! ;

The good nights are not made for sleep, nor the good days for dreaming in,

    And at the end in the big Circus tent we sat and shook and stewed like sin!


    Some children there had got - but where?

Sent from the south, perhaps - a red bouquet

    Of roses, sweetening the fetid air

With scent from gardens by some far away blue bay.

    They threw one at the dancing bear;

The white clown caught it. From St. Rémy's tower

    The deep, slow bell tolled out the hour;

The black clown, with his dirty grin

    Lay, sprawling in the dust, as She rode in.


She stood on a white horse-and suddenly you saw the bend

    Of a far-off road at dawn, with knights riding by,

A field of spears - and then the gallant day

Go out in storm, with ragged clouds low down, sullen and grey

    Against red heavens: wild and awful, such a sky

    As witnesses against you at the end

Of a great battle; bugles blowing, blood and dust -

The old *Morte d'Arthur*, fight you must -.

It died in anger. But it was not death
That had you by the throat, stopping your breath.
She looked like Victory. She rode my way.

She laughed at the black clown and then she flew
      A bird above us, on the wing
Of her white arms; and you saw through
A rent in the old tent, a patch of sky
With one dim star. She flew, but not so high -
      And then she did not fly;
She stood in the bright moonlight at the door
Of a strange room, she threw her slippers on the floor -
         Again, again
      You heard the patter of the rain,
      The starving rain - it was this Thing,
Summer was this, the gold mist in your eyes;-
        Oh God! it dies,
        But after death-,
   To-night the splendour and the sting
   Blows back and catches at your breath,
The smell of beasts, the smell of dust, the scent of all the roses in the world, the sea, the Spring,
The beat of drums, the pad of hoofs, music, the dream, the dream, the Enchanted Thing!

   At first you scarcely saw her face,

You knew the maddening feet were there,
What called was that half-hidden, white unrest
To which now and then she pressed
    Her finger-tips; but as she slackened pace
    And turned and looked at you it grew quite bare:
        There was not anything you did not dare: -
Like trumpeters the hours passed until the last day of the Fair.

    In the *Place d'Armes* all afternoon
    The building birds had sung "Soon, soon",
The shuttered streets slept sound that night,
    It was full moon:
The path into the wood was almost white,
The trees were very still and seemed to stare:
    Not far before your soul the Dream flits on,
    But when you touch it, it is gone
And quite alone your soul stands there.

Mother of Christ, no one has seen your eyes: how can men pray
    Even unto you?
There were only wolves' eyes in the wood -
    My Mother is a woman too:
Nothing is true that is not good,
With that quick smile of hers, I have heard her say; -
I wish I had gone back home to-day;
    I should have watched the light that so gently dies

From our high window, in the Paris skies,
    The long, straight chain
    Of lamps hung out along the Seine:
I would have turned to her and let the rain
Beat on her breast as it does against the pane;-
    Nothing will be the same again; -
There is something strange in my little Mother's eyes,
There is something new in the old heavenly air of Spring -
The smell of beasts, the smell of dust - The Enchanted Thing!

All my life long I shall see moonlight on the fern
    And the black trunks of trees. Only the hair
Of any woman can belong to God.
The stalks are cruelly broken where we trod,
      There had been violets there,
      I shall not care
As I used to do when I see the bracken burn.

# Beside the Bed

Someone has shut the shining eyes, straightened and folded
   The wandering hands quietly covering the unquiet breast:
So, smoothed and silenced you lie, like a child, not again to be questioned or scolded
   But, for you, not one of us believes that this is rest.

Not so to close the windows down can cloud and deaden
   The blue beyond: or to screen the wavering flame subdue its breath:
Why, if I lay my cheek to your cheek, your grey lips, like dawn, would quiver and redden.
   Breaking into the old, odd smile at this fraud of death.

Because all night you have not turned to us or spoken
   It is time for you to wake ; your dreams were never very deep :
I, for one, have seen the thin, bright, twisted threads of them dimmed suddenly and broken.
   This is only a most piteous pretence of sleep!

# In Nunhead Cemetery

It is the clay what makes the earth stick to his spade;
    He fills in holes like this year after year;
The others have gone; they were tired, and half afraid
    But I would rather be standing here;

There is nowhere else to go. I have seen this place
    From the windows of the train that's going past
Against the sky. This is rain on my face -
    It was raining here when I saw it last.

There is something horrible about a flower;
    This, broken in my hand, is one of those
He threw it in just now; it will not live another hour;
    There are thousands more; you do not miss a rose.

One of the children hanging about
    Pointed at the whole dreadful heap and smiled
This morning after THAT was carried out;
    There is something terrible about a child.

We were like children last week, in the Strand;
    That was the day you laughed at me
Because I tried to make you understand
    The cheap, stale chap I used to be
    Before I saw the things you made me see.

This is not a real place; perhaps by-and-by
    I shall wake - I am getting drenched with all this rain:
To-morrow I will tell you about the eyes of the Crystal Palace train
    Looking down on us, and you will laugh and I shall see what you see again.

    Not here, not now. We said "Not yet
    Across our low stone parapet
Will the quick shadows of the sparrows fall.

    But still it was a lovely thing
    Through the grey months to wait for Spring
    With the birds that go a-gypsying
In the parks till the blue seas call.
    And next to these, you used to care
    For the Lions in Trafalgar Square,
Who'll stand and speak for London when her bell of Judgement tolls -
    And the gulls at Westminster that were
    The old sea-captains souls.
To-day again the brown tide splashes step by step, the river stair,
    And the gulls are there!

By a month we have missed our Day:
    The children would have hung about
Round the carriage and over the way
    As you and I came out.

We should have stood on the gulls' black cliffs and heard the sea
    And seen the moon's white track,
I would have called, you would have come to me
    And kissed me back.

You have never done that: I do not know
    Why I stood staring at your bed
And heard you, though you spoke so low,
    But could not reach your hands, your little head;
There was nothing we could not do, you said,
    And you went, and I let you go!

Now I will burn you back, I will burn you through,
    Though I am damned for it we two will lie
    And burn, here where the starlings fly
    To these white stones from the wet sky - ;
    Dear, you will say this is not I -
It would not be you, it would not be you!

If for only a little while
    You will think of it you will understand,
If you will touch my sleeve and smile

As you did that morning in the Strand
I can wait quietly with you
Or go away if you want me to -
God! What is God? but your face has gone and your hand!
Let me stay here too.

When I was quite a little lad
At Christmas time we went half mad
For joy of all the toys we had,
And then we used to sing about the sheep
The shepherds watched by night;
We used to pray to Christ to keep
Our small souls safe till morning light - ;
I am scared, I am staying with you to-night -
Put me to sleep.

I shall stay here: here you can see the sky;
The houses in the street are much too high;
There is no one left to speak to there;
Here they are everywhere,
And just above them fields and fields of roses lie -
If he would dig it all up again they would not die.

# The Peddler

Lend me, a little while, the key
   That locks your heavy heart, and I'll give you back -
Rarer than books and ribbons and beads bright to see,
   This little Key of Dreams out of my pack.

The road, the road, beyond men's bolted doors,
   There shall I walk and you go free of me,
For yours lies North across the moors,
   And mine lies South. To what seas?

How if we stopped and let our solemn selves go by,
   While my gay ghost caught and kissed yours, as ghosts don't do,
And by the wayside, this forgotten you and I
   Sat, and were twenty-two?

Give me the key that locks your tired eyes,
   And I will lend you this one from my pack,
Brighter than coloured beads and painted books that make men wise:
   Take it. No, give it back!

## Pêcheresse

Down the long quay the slow boats glide,
   While here and there a house looms white
Against the gloom of the waterside,
   And some high window throws a light
   As they sail out into the night.

At dawn they will bring in again
   To women knitting on the quay
Who wait for him, their man of men;
   I stand with them, and watch the sea
   Which may have taken mine from me.

Just so the long days come and go.
   The nights, ma Doué! the nights are cold!
Our Lady's heart is as frozen snow,
   Since this one sin I have not told;
   And I shall die or perhaps grow old

Before he comes. The foreign ships
   Bring many a one of face and name
As strange as his, to buy your lips,
   A gold piece for a scarlet shame
   Like mine. But mine was not the same.

One night was ours, one short grey day
   Of sudden sin, unshrived, untold.
He found me, and I lost the way
   To Paradise for him. I sold
   My soul for love and not for gold

He bought my soul, but even so,

My face is all that he has seen,
His is the only face I know,
And in the dark church, like a screen.
   It shuts God out; it comes between;

While in some narrow foreign street
   Or loitering on the crowded quay,
Who knows what others he may meet
   To turn his eyes away from me?
   Many are fair to such as he!

There is but one for such as I
   To love, to hate, to hunger for;
I shall, perhaps, grow old and die,
   With one short day to spend and store,
   One night, in all my life, no more.

Just so the long days come and go,
   Yet this one sin I will not tell
Though Mary's heart is as frozen snow
And all nights are cold for one warmed too well.
   But, oh! ma Doué! *the nights of Hell!*

# The Changeling

Toll no bell for me, dear Father, dear Mother,
    Waste no sighs;
There are my sisters, there is my little brother
    Who plays in the place called Paradise,
Your children all, your children for ever;
    But I, so wild,
Your disgrace, with the queer brown face, was never,
    Never, I know, but half your child!

In the garden at play, all day, last summer,
    Far and away I heard
The sweet "tweet-tweet" of a strange new-comer,
    The dearest, clearest call of a bird.
It lived down there in the deep green hollow,
    My own old home, and the fairies say
The word of a bird is a thing to follow,
    So I was away a night and a day.

One evening, too, by the nursery fire,
    We snuggled close and sat round so still,
When suddenly as the wind blew higher,
    Something scratched on the window-sill.
A pinched brown face peered in – I shivered;
    No one listened or seemed to see;
The arms of it waved and the wings of it quivered,
    Whoo – I knew it had come for me;
    Some are as bad as bad can be!

All night long they danced in the rain,
Round and round in a dripping chain,
Threw their caps at the window-pane,
    Tried to make me scream and shout

    And fling the bedclothes all about:
I meant to stay in bed that night,
And if only you had left a light
    They would never have got me out.

    Sometimes I wouldn't speak, you see,
    Or answer when you spoke to me,
Because in the long, still dusks of Spring
You can hear the whole world whispering:
    The shy green grasses making love,
    The feathers grow on the dear, grey dove,
    The tiny heart of the redstart beat,
    The patter of the squirrel's feet,
The pebbles pushing in the silver streams,
The rushes talking in their dreams,
    The swish-swish of the bat's black wings,
    The wild-wood bluebell's sweet ting-tings,
    Humming and hammering at your ear,
      Everything there is to hear
In the heart of hidden things,
    But not in the midst of the nursery riot.
    That's why I wanted to be quiet,
      Couldn't do my sums, or sing,
      Or settle down to anything.
    And when, for that, I was sent upstairs
    I did kneel down to say my prayers;
But the King who sits on your high church steeple
Has nothing to do with us fairy people!

'Times I pleased you, dear Father, dear Mother,
    Learned all my lessons and liked to play,
And dearly I loved the little pale brother
    Whom some other bird must have called away.
Why did They bring me here to make me

    Not quite bad and not quite good,
Why, unless They're wicked, do They want, in spite, to take me
      Back to their wet, wild wood?

Now, every night I shall see the windows shining,
    The gold lamp's glow, and the fire's red gleam,
While the best of us are twining twigs and the rest of us are whining
      In the hollow by the stream.
Black and chill are Their nights on the wold;
    And They live so long and They feel no pain:
I shall grow up, but never grow old,
I shall always, always be very cold,
      I shall never come back again!


**Ken**

The town is old and very steep,
   A place of bells and cloisters and grey towers,
And black clad people walking in their sleep -
   A nun, a priest, a woman taking flowers
   To her new grave; and watched from end to end
     By the great Church above, through the still hours:
      But in the morning and the early dark
The children wake to dart from doors and call
Down the wide, crooked street, where, at the bend,
    Before it climbs up to the park,
Ken's is the gabled house facing the Castle wall.

When first I came upon him there
Suddenly, on the half-lit stair,
I think I hardly found a trace
Of likeness to a human face
   In his. And I said then
If in His image God made men,

Some other must have made poor Ken -
But for his eyes which looked at you
As two red, wounded stars might do.

He scarcely spoke, you scarcely heard,
    His voice broke off in little jars
To tears sometimes. An uncouth bird
   He seemed as he ploughed up the street,
Groping, with knarred, high-lifted feet
   And arms thrust out as if to beat
     Always against a threat of bars.

And oftener than not there'd be
   A child just higher than his knee
Trotting beside him. Through his dim
   Long twilight this, at least, shone clear,
   That all the children and the deer,
     Whom every day he went to see
Out in the park, belonged to him.

    "God help the folk that next him sits
     He fidgets so, with his poor wits."
The neighbours said on Sunday nights
When he would go to Church to "see the lights!"
   Although for these he used to fix
   His eyes upon a crucifix
   In a dark corner, staring on
   Till everybody else had gone.
   And sometimes, in his evil fits,
You could not move him from his chair -
You did not look at him as he sat there,
   Biting his rosary to bits.
While pointing to the Christ he tried to say
    "Take it away."

      Nothing was dead:
He said "a bird" if he picked up a broken wing,
    A perished leaf or any such thing
      Was just "a rose"; and once when I had said
  He must not stand and knock there anymore,
  He left a twig on the mat outside my door.

    Not long ago
The last thrush stiffened in the snow,
  While black against a sullen sky
  The sighing pines stood by.
But now the wind has left our rattled pane
To flutter the hedge-sparrow's wing,
The birches in the wood are red again
    And only yesterday
The larks went up a little way to sing
    What lovers say
  Who loiter in the lanes today;
  The buds begin to talk of May
With learned rooks on city trees,
    And if God please
    With all of these
We too, shall see another Spring.

But in that red brick barn upon the hill
  I wonder - can one own the deer,
And does one walk with children still
    As one did here -
      Do roses grow
  Beneath those twenty windows in a row -
    And if some night
When you have not seen any light
They cannot move you from your chair

    What happens there?
    I do not know.

    So, when they took
Ken to that place, I did not look
        After he called and turned on me His eyes.
    These I shall see -

## A Quoi Bon Dire

    Seventeen years ago you said
Something that sounded like Good-bye:
    And everybody thinks you are dead
        But I.

    So I as I grow stiff and cold
To this and that say Good-bye too;
    And everybody sees that I am old
        But you.

    And one fine morning in a sunny lane
Some boy and girl will meet and kiss and swear
    That nobody can love their way again
        While over there
You will have smiled, and I shall have tossed your hair

## The Quiet House

When we were children Old Nurse used to say
    The house was like an auction or a fair
    Until the lot of us were safe in bed.
    It has been quiet as the country-side
    Since Ted and Janey and then Mother died
And Tom crossed Father and was sent away.
After the lawsuit he could not hold up his head,
    Poor father, and he does not care
    For people here, or to go anywhere.

To get away to Aunt's for that week-end
    Was hard enough; (since then, a year ago,
    He scarcely lets me slip out of his sight)
At first I did not like my cousin's friend,
    I did not think I should remember him:
    His voice has gone, his face is growing dim
And if I like him now I do not know.
    He frightened me before he smiled -
    He did not ask me if he might -
    He said that he would come one Sunday night,
    He spoke to me as if I were a child.

No year has been like this that has just gone by;
    It may be that what Father says is true,
If things are so it does not matter why:
    But everything has burned and not quite through.

   The colours of the world have turned
    To flame, the blue, the gold has burned
In what used to be such a leaden sky.
When you are burned quite through you die.

   Red is the strangest pain to bear;
In Spring the leaves on the budding trees;
In Summer the roses are worse than these,
   More terrible than they are sweet:
   A rose can stab you across the street
    Deeper than any knife:
   And the crimson haunts you everywhere –
Thin shafts of sunlight, like the ghosts of reddened swords
              have struck our stair
As if, coming down, you had split your life.

   I think that my soul is red
Like the soul of a sword or a scarlet flower:
   But when these are dead
   They have had their hour.

   I shall have had mine, too,
    For from head to feet,
   I am burned and stabbed half through,
    And the pain is deadly sweet.

   Then things that kill us seem
    Blind to the death they give:

   It is only in our dream
     The things that kill us live.

The room is shut where Mother died,
   The other rooms are as they were,
The world goes on the same outside,
   The sparrows fly across the Square,
   The children play as we four did there,
   The trees grow green and brown and bare,
The sun shines on the dead Church spire,
   And nothing lives here but the fire,

While Father watches from his chair
         Day follows day
The same, or now and then, a different grey,
         Till, like his hair,
Which Mother said was wavy once and bright,
         They will all turn white.

   To-night I heard a bell again -
Outside it was the same mist of fine rain,
The lamps just lighted down the long, dim street,
         No one for me -
   I think it is myself I go there to meet:
I do not care; someday I SHALL not think; I shall not BE!

## On the Asylum Road

Theirs is the house whose windows—every pane—
   Are made of darkly stained or clouded glass:
Sometimes you come upon them in the lane,
   The saddest crowd that you will ever pass.

But still we merry town or village folk
   Throw to their scattered stare a kindly grin,
And think no shame to stop and crack a joke
   With the incarnate wages of man's sin.

None but ourselves in our long gallery we meet,
   The moor-hen stepping from her reeds with dainty feet,
     The hare-bell bowing on his stem,
Dance not with us; their pulses beat
   To fainter music; nor do we to them
      Make their life sweet.

The gayest crowd that they will ever pass
   Are we to brother-shadows in the lane:
Our windows, too, are clouded glass
   To them, yes, every pane!

## Jour des Morts

(Cimetière Montparnasse)


Sweetheart, is this the last of all our posies,
   And little festivals, my flowers are they
But white and wistful ghosts of gayer roses
   Shut with you in this grim garden? Not to-day,
Ah! no! come out with me before the grey gate closes
   It is your fête and here is your bouquet.


## The Forest Road

The forest road,
The infinite straight road stretching away
World without end: the breathless road between the walls
Of the black listening trees: the hushed, grey road
Beyond the window that you shut to-night
Crying that you would look at it by day -
There is a shadow there that sings and calls
But not for you. Oh! hidden eyes that plead in sleep
Against the lonely dark, if I could touch the fear
And leave it kissed away on quiet lids -
If I could hush these hands that are half-awake,
Groping for me in sleep I could go free.
I wish that God would take them out of mine

And fold them like the wings of frightened birds

Shot cruelly down, but fluttering into quietness so soon.

Broken, forgotten things? There is no grief for them in the green Spring

When the new birds fly back to the old trees.

But it shall not be so with you. I will look back. I wish I knew that God would stand

Smiling and looking down on you when morning comes,

To hold you, when you wake, closer than I,

So gently though: and not with famished lips or hungry arms:

He does not hurt the frailest, dearest things

As we do in the dark. See, dear, your hair -

I must unloose this hair that sleeps and dreams

About my face, and clings like the brown weed

To drowned, delivered things, tossed by the tired sea

Back to the beaches. Oh! your hair! If you had lain

A long time dead on the rough, glistening ledge

Of some black cliff, forgotten by the tide,

The raving winds would tear, the dripping brine would rust away

Fold after fold of all the loveliness

That wraps you round, and makes you, lying here,

The passionate fragrance that the roses are.

But death would spare the glory of your head

In the long sweetness of the hair that does not die:

The spray would leap to it in every storm,

The scent of the unsilenced sea would linger on

In these dark waves, and round the silence that was you -

Only the nesting gulls would hear - but there would still be whispers in your hair;

Keep them for me; keep them for me. What is this singing on the road

That makes all other music like the music in a dream -

Dumb to the dancing and the marching feet; you know, in dreams, you see

Old pipers playing that you cannot hear,

And ghostly drums that only seem to beat. This seems to climb:

Is it the music of a larger place? It makes our room too small: it is like a stair,

A calling stair that climbs up to a smile you scarcely see,

Dim, but so waited for; and you know what a smile is, how it calls,

How if I smiled you always ran to me.

Now you must sleep forgetfully, as children do.

There is a Spirit sits by us in sleep

Nearer than those who walk with us in the bright day.

I think he has a tranquil, saving face: I think he came

Straight from the hills: he may have suffered there in time gone by,

And once, from those forsaken heights, looked down,

Lonely himself, on all the lonely sorrows of the earth.

It is his kingdom - Sleep. If I could leave you there -

If, without waking you, I could get up and reach the door -!

We used to go together. - Shut, scared eyes,

Poor, desolate, desperate hands, it is not I

Who thrust you off. No, take your hands away -

I cannot strike your lonely hands. Yes, I have struck your heart,
It did not come so near. Then lie you there
Dear and wild heart behind this quivering snow
With two red stains on it: and I will strike and tear
Mine out, and scatter it to yours. Oh! throbbing dust,
You that were life, our little wind-blown hearts!

        The road! the road!
There is a shadow there: I see my soul,
I hear my soul, singing among the trees!


## Madeleine in Church

Here, in the darkness, where this plaster saint
Stands nearer than God stands to our distress.
And one small candle shines, but not so faint
As the far lights of everlastingness
I'd rather kneel than over there, in open day
Where Christ is hanging, rather pray
To something more like my own clay,
Not too divine;
For, once, perhaps my little saint
Before he got his niche and crown,
Had one short stroll about the town ;
It brings him closer, just that taint

And anyone can wash the paint
Off our poor faces, his and mine!

Is that why I see Monty now? equal to any saint, poor boy, as good as gold.
But still, with just the proper trace
Of earthliness on his shining wedding face;
And then gone suddenly blank and old
The hateful day of the divorce:
Stuart got his, hands down, of course
Crowing like twenty cocks and grinning like a horse:
But Monty took it hard. All said and done I liked him best, —
He was the first, he stands out clearer than the rest.
It seems too funny all we other rips
Should have immortal souls; Monty and Redge quite damnably
Keep theirs afloat while we go down like scuttled ships. —
It's funny too, how easily we sink.
One might put up a monument, I think
To half the world and cut across it "Lost at Sea!"
I should drown Jim, poor little sparrow, if I netted him to-night —
No, it's no use this penny light —
Or my poor saint with his tin-pot crown —
The trees of Calvary are where they were,
When we are sure that we can spare
The tallest, let us go and strike it down
And leave the other two still standing there.

I, too, would ask Him to remember me

If there were any Paradise beyond this earth that I could see.

Oh! quiet Christ who never knew

The poisonous fangs that bite us through

And make us do the things we do.

See how we suffer and fight and die,

How helpless and how low we lie,

God holds You, and You hang so high,

Though no one looking long at You,

Can think You do not suffer too,

But, up there, from your still, star-lighted tree

What can You know, what can You really see

Of this dark ditch, the soul of me!

We are what we are: when I was half a child I could not sit

Watching black shadows on green lawns and red carnations burning in the sun.

Without paying so heavily for it

That joy and pain, like any mother and her unborn child were almost one.

I could hardly bear

The dreams upon the eyes of white geraniums in the dusk,

The thick, close voice of musk,

The jessamine music on the thin night air.

Or, sometimes, my own hands about me anywhere —

The sight of my own face (for it was lovely then) even the scent of my own hair,
Oh! there was nothing, nothing that did not sweep to the high seat
Of laughing gods, and then blow down and beat
My soul into the highway dust, as hoofs do the dropped roses of the street.
I think my body was my soul,
And when we are made thus
Who shall control
Our hands, our eyes, the wandering passion of our feet.
Who shall teach us
To thrust the world out of our heart; to say, till perhaps in death,
When the race is run.
And it is forced from us with our last breath
"Thy will be done"?
If it is Your will that we should be content with the tame, bloodless things.
As pale as angels smirking by, with folded wings.
Oh ! I know Virtue, and the peace it brings!
The temperate, well-worn smile
The one man gives you, when you are evermore his own:
And afterwards the child's, for a little while,
With its unknowing and all-seeing eyes
So soon to change, and make you feel how quick
The clock goes round. If one had learned the trick —
(How does one though?) quite early on,

Of long green pastures under placid skies.
One might be walking now with patient truth.
What did we ever care for it, who have asked for youth,
When, oh! my God! this is going or has gone?

There is a portrait of my mother, at nineteen.
With the black spaniel, standing by the garden seat,
The dainty head held high against the painted green
And throwing out the youngest smile, shy, but half haughty and half sweet.
Her picture then: but simply Youth, or simply Spring
To me to-day: a radiance on the wall.
So exquisite, so heart-breaking a thing
Beside the mask that I remember, shrunk and small,
Sapless and lined like a dead leaf,
All that was left of oh! the loveliest face, by time and grief!

And in the glass, last night, I saw a ghost behind my chair —
Yet why remember it, when one can still go moderately gay — ?
Or could — with any one of the old 'crew,
But oh! these boys! the solemn way
They take you, and the things they say —
This "I have only as long as you"
When you remind them you are not precisely twenty- two —
Although at heart perhaps — God! if it were
Only the face, only the hair!

If Jim had written to me as he did to-day
A year ago — and now it leaves me cold —
I know what this means, old, old, old!
Et avec ça — mais on a vécu, tout se paie.

That is not always true: there was my Mother — (well at least the dead are free!)
Yoked to the man that Father was; yoked to the woman I am, Monty too;
The little portress at the Convent School, stewing in hell so patiently;
The poor, fair boy who shot himself at Aix. And what of me — and what of me?
But I, I paid for what I had, and they for nothing. No, one cannot see
How it shall be made up to them in some serene eternity.
If there were fifty heavens God could not give us back the child who went or never came;
Here, on our little patch of this great earth, the sun of any darkened day.
Not one of all the starry buds hung on the hawthorn trees of last year's May,
No shadow from the sloping fields of yesterday;
For every hour they slant across the hedge a different way,
The shadows are never the same.

"Find rest in Him" One knows the parsons' tags —

Back to the fold, across the evening fields, like any flock of baa-ing sheep:
Yes, it may be, when He has shorn, led us to slaughter, torn the bleating soul in us to rags,
For so lie giveth His beloved sleep.
Oh! He will take us stripped and done,
Driven into His heart. So we are won:
Then safe, safe are we? in the shelter of His everlasting wings —
I do not envy Him his victories. His arms are full of broken things.

But I shall not be in them. Let Him take
The finer ones, the easier to break.
And they are not gone, yet, for me, the lights, the colours, the perfumes,
Though now they speak rather in sumptuous rooms.
In silks and in gem-like wines;
Here, even, in this corner where my little candle shines
And overhead the lancet-window glows
With golds and crimsons you could almost drink
To know how jewels taste, just as I used to think
There was the scent in every red and yellow rose
Of all the sunsets. But this place is grey,
And much too quiet. No one here.
Why, this is awful, this is fear!
Nothing to see, no face.
Nothing to hear except your heart beating in space

As if the world was ended. Dead at last!

Dead soul, dead body, tied together fast.

These to go on with and alone, to the slow end:

No one to sit with, really, or to speak to, friend to friend:

Out of the long procession, black or white or red

Not one left now to say "Still I am here, then see you, dear, lay here your head."

Only the doll's house looking on the Park

To-night, all nights, I know, when the man puts the lights out, very dark.

With, upstairs, in the blue and gold box of a room, just the maids' footsteps overhead.

Then utter silence and the empty world — the room — the bed —

The corpse! No, not quite dead, while this cries out in me.

But nearly: very soon to be

A handful of forgotten dust —

There must be someone. Christ! there must,

Tell me there will be someone. Who?

If there were no one else, could it be You?


How old was Mary out of whom you cast

So many devils? Was she young or perhaps for years

She had sat staring, with dry eyes, at this and that man going past

Till suddenly she saw You on the steps of Simon's house

And stood and looked at You through tears.

I think she must have known by those

The thing, for what it was that had come to her.

For some of us there is a passion, I suppose

So far from earthly cares and earthly fears

That in its stillness you can hardly stir

Or in its nearness, lift your hand.

So great that you have simply got to stand

Looking at it through tears, through tears

Then straight from these there broke the kiss,

I think You must have known by this

The thing, for what it was, that had come to You:

She did not love You like the rest.

It was in her own way, but at the worst, the best,

She gave you something altogether new.

And through it all , from her, no word,

She scarcely saw You, scarcely heard:

Surely You knew when she so touched You with her hair.

Or by the wet cheek lying there,

And while her perfume clung to You from head to feet all through the day

That You can change the things for which we care.

But even You, unless You kill us, not the way.


This, then was peace for her, but passion too.

I wonder was it like a kiss that once I knew,

The only one that I would care to take

Into the grave with me, to which if there were afterwards, to wake.

Almost as happy as the carven dead
In some dim chancel lying head by head
We slept with it, but face to face, the whole night through —
One breath, one throbbing quietness, as if the thing behind our lips was endless life,
Lost, as I woke, to hear in the strange earthly dawn, his "Are you there?"
And lie still, listening to the wind outside, among the firs.

So Mary chose the dream of Him for what was left to her of night and day,
It is the only truth: it is the dream in us that neither life nor death nor any other thing
can take away :
But if she had not touched Him in the doorway of the dream could she have cared so much?
She was a sinner, we are what we are: the spirit afterwards, but first, the touch.
And He has never shared with me my haunted house beneath the trees
Of Eden and Calvary, with its ghosts that have not any eyes for tears,
And the happier guests who would not see, or if they did, remember these.
Though they lived there a thousand years.
Outside, too gravely looking at me. He seems to stand.
And looking at Him, if my forgotten spirit came
Unwillingly back, what could it claim

Of those calm eyes, that quiet speech.

Breaking like a slow tide upon the beach.

The scarred, not quite human hand? —

Unwillingly back to the burden of old imaginings

When it has learned so long not to think, not to be,

Again, again it would speak as it has spoken to me of things

That I shall not see !

I cannot bear to look at this divinely bent and gracious head :

When I was small I never quite believed that He was dead :

And at the Convent school I used to lie awake in bed

Thinking about His hands. It did not matter what they said,

He was alive to me, so hurt, so hurt! And most of all in Holy Week

When there was no one else to see

I used to think it would not hurt me too, so terribly.

If He had ever seemed to notice me

Or, if, for once, He would only speak.

## Exspecto Resurrectionem

    Oh ! King who hast the key

    Of that dark room.

The last which prisons us but held not Thee

    Thou know'st its gloom.

  Dost Thou a little love this one

    Shut in to-night,

  Young and so piteously alone,

    Cold - out of sight?

Thou know'st how hard and bare

The pillow of that new-made narrow bed.

    Then leave not there

    So dear a head!

## On the Road to the Sea

We passed each other, turned and stopped for half an hour, then went our way,
    I who make other women smile did not make you -
But no man can move mountains in a day.
    So this hard thing is yet to do.

But first I want your life: -before I die I want to see
    The world that lies behind the strangeness of your eyes,
There is nothing gay or green there for my gathering, it may be,
      Yet on brown fields there lies
A haunting purple bloom: is there not something in grey skies
        And in grey sea?
    I want what world there is behind your eyes,
    I want your life and you will not give it me.

    Now, if I look, I see you walking down the years,
    Young, and through August fields -a face, a thought, a swinging
dream perched on a stile;
    I would have liked (so vile we are!) to have taught you tears
        But most to have made you smile.

    To-day is not enough or yesterday: God sees it all -
Your length on sunny lawns, the wakeful rainy nights; tell me;
(how vain to ask), but it is not a question - just a call;

Show me then, only your notched inches climbing up the garden wall,
        I like you best when you are small.


      Is this a stupid thing to say
      Not having spent with you one day?
No matter; I shall never touch your hair
Or hear the little tick behind your breast,
      Still it is there,
      And as a flying bird
Brushes the branches where it may not rest
      I have brushed your hand and heard
The child in you: I like that best
So small, so dark, so sweet; and were you also then too grave and wise?
   Always I think. Then put your far off little hand in mine; Oh! let it rest;
I will not stare into the early world beyond the opening eyes,
   Or vex or scare what I love best.
   But I want your life before mine bleeds away -
     Here -not in heavenly hereafters -soon, -
     I want your smile this very afternoon,
   (The last of all my vices, pleasant people used to say,
     I wanted and I sometimes got -the Moon!)


     You know, at dusk, the last bird's cry,
   And round the house the flap of the bat's low flight,
     Trees that go black against the sky

And then -how soon the night!


   No shadow of you on any bright road again,
And at the darkening end of this -what voice? whose kiss? As if you'd say!
It is not I who have walked with you, it will not be I who take away
   Peace, peace, my little handful of the gleaner's grain
   From your reaped fields at the shut of day.


      Peace! Would you not rather die
     Reeling, -with all the cannons at your ear?
        So, at least, would I,
   And I may not be here
   To-night, to-morrow morning or next year.
   Still I will let you keep your life a little while,
        See dear?
    *I have made you smile.*


## The Sunlit House

White, through the gate it gleamed and slept
   In shattered sunshine. The parched garden flowers
Their scarlet petals from the beds unswept
   Like children unloved and ill-kept
      Dreamed through the hours

Two blue hydrangeas by the blistered door burned brown
    Watched there, and no one in the town
    Cared to go past it night or day
    Though why this was they wouldn't say
But I, the stranger, knew that I must stay.
    Pace up the weed-grown paths and down -
    Till one afternoon - there is just a doubt -
    But I fancy I heard a tiny shout -
    From an upper window a bird flew out -
        And I went my way.


## The Shade-Catchers

I think they were about as high
As haycocks are. They went running by
Catching bits of shade in the sunny street :
  "I've got one," cried sister to brother.
"I've got two." "Now I've got another."
But scudding away on their little bare feet,
They left the shade in the sunny street.

## Le Sacré-Coeur
(Montmartre)

It is dark up here on the heights,
Between the dome and the stars it is quiet too,
While down there under the crowded Heights

Flares the importunate face of you.
Dear Paris of the hot white hands, the scarlet lips, the scented hair,
Une jolie fille a vendre, tres cher ;
A thing of gaiety, a thing of sorrow.
Bought to-night, possessed, and tossed
Back to the mart again to-morrow.
Worth and over, what you cost ;
While half your charm is that you are
Withal, like some unpurchasable star,

So old, so young and infinite and lost.

It is dark on the dome-capped hill,

Serenely dark, divinely still,
Yet here is the Man who bought you first

Dying of his immortal smart.
Your Lover, the King with the broken heart.
Who while you, feasting, drink your fill.
Pass round the cup
Not looking up.
Calls down to you, "I thirst."

"A king with a broken heart ! Mon Dieu!

One breaks so many, cela pent se croire,

To remember all c'est la mer a boire,

And the first, mais comme c'est vieux.
Perhaps there is still some keepsake — or

One has possibly sold it for a song:
On ne pent pas toujoiirs pleurer les morts,

And this One — He has been dead so long! "

## Song

   Love love to-day, my dear

   Love is not always here

Wise maids know how soon grows sere

     The greenest leaf of Spring.

        But no man knoweth

        Whither it goeth

        When the wind bloweth

          So frail a thing.


   Love love, my dear, to-day

   If the ship's in the bay

If the bird has come your way

     That sings on summer trees.

        When his song faileth

        And the ship saileth

        No voice availeth

          To call back these.

# Saturday Market

Bury your heart in some deep green hollow
    Or hide it up in a kind old tree;
Better still, give it the swallow
    When she goes over the sea.

In Saturday's Market there's eggs a 'plenty
    And dead-alive ducks with their legs tied down,
Grey old gaffers and boys of twenty—
    Girls and the women of the town—
Pitchers and sugar-sticks, ribbons and laces,
    Poises and whips and dicky-birds' seed,
Silver pieces and smiling faces,
    In Saturday Market they've all they need.

What were you showing in Saturday Market
    That set it grinning from end to end
Girls and gaffers and boys of twenty?
    Cover it close with your shawl, my friend -
Hasten you home with the laugh behind you,
    Over the down - out of sight,
Fasten your door, though no one will find you,
    No one will look on a Market night.

See, you, the shawl is wet, take out from under

    The red dead thing—. In the white of the moon
On the flags does it stir again? Well, and no wonder!
    Best make an end of it; bury it soon.
If there is blood on the hearth who'll know it?
    Or blood on the stairs,
When a murder is over and done why show it?
    In Saturday Market nobody cares.

Then lie you straight on your bed for a short, short weeping
    And still, for a long, long rest,
There's never a one in the town so sure of sleeping
    As you, in the house on the down with a hole in your breast.

        Think no more of the swallow,
            Forget, you, the sea,
    Never again remember the deep green hollow
            Or the top of the kind old tree!

## Arracombe Wood

    Some said, because he wud'n spaik
    Any words to women but Yes and No,
Nor put out his hand for Parson to shake
    He mun be bird-witted. But I do go
    By the lie of the barley that he did sow,
And I wish for no better thing than to hold a rake
    Like Dave, in his time, or to see him mow.

    Put up in the churchyard a month ago,
'A bitter old soul,' they said, but i wadn't so.
His heart were in Arracombe Wood where he'd used to go
To sit and talk wi' his shadder till sun went low,
Thought what it was all about us'll never know.
    And there baint no mem'ry in the place
    Of th' old man's footmark, nor his face;
    Arracombe Wood do think more of a crow -
'Will be violets there in the Spring: in Summer time the spider's lace;
    And come the Fall, the whizzle and race
Of the dry, dead leaves when the wind gives chase;
    And on the Eve of Christmas, fallin' snow.

## Sea Love

Tide be runnin' the great world over:
    'Twas only last June month I mind that we
Was thinkin' the toss and the call in the breast of the lover
    So everlastin' as the sea.

Heer's the same little fishes that sputter an swim,
    Wi' the moon's old glim on the grey, wet sand;
An' him no more to me nor me to him
    Than the wind goin' over my hand.

## The Road to Kerity

Do you remember the two old people we passed
on the road to Kerity,
Resting their sack on the stones, by the drenched wayside,
Looking at us with their lightless eyes
through the driving rain, and then out again
To the rocks, and the long white line of the tide:
Frozen ghosts that were children once,
husband and wife, father, and mother,
Looking at us with those frozen eyes;
have you ever seen anything quite so chilled
or so old?
But we – with our arms about each other,

We did not feel the cold!

## I Have Been through the Gates

His heart to me, was a place of palaces and pinnacles and shining towers;
I saw it then as we see things in dreams, -I do not remember how long I slept;
I remember the tress, and the high, white walls, and how the sun was always on the towers;
The walls are standing to-day, and the gates; I have been through the gates, I have groped, I have crept
Back, back. There is dust in the streets, and blood; they are empty; darkness is over them;
His heart is a place with the lights gone out, forsaken by great winds and the heavenly rain, unclean and unswept,
Like the heart of the holy city, old blind, beautiful Jerusalem;
        Over which Christ wept.

## The Cenotaph

Not yet will those measureless fields be green again
Where only yesterday the wild sweet blood of wonderful youth was shed;
There is a grave whose earth must hold too long, too deep a stain,
Though forever over it we may speak as proudly as we may tread.
But here, where the watchers by lonely hearths from the thrust of an inward sword have more slowly bled,
We shall build the Cenotaph: Victory, winged, with Peace, winged too, at the column's head.
And over the stairway, at the foot --oh! here, leave desolate, passionate hands to spread
Violets, roses, and laurel with the small sweet twinkling country things
Speaking so wistfully of other Springs
From the little gardens of little places where son or sweetheart was born and bred.
In splendid sleep, with a thousand brothers
    To lovers --to mothers
    Here, too, lies he:
Under the purple, the green, the red,
It is all young life: it must break some women's hearts to see
Such a brave, gay coverlet to such a bed!
Only, when all is done and said,
God is not mocked and neither are the dead.
For this will stand in our Market-place --
    Who'll sell, who'll buy
    (Will you or I
Lie each to each with the better grace)?
While looking into every busy whore's and huckster's face
As they drive their bargains, is the Face
Of God: and some young, piteous, murdered face.

## In The Fields

Lord when I look at lovely things which pass,
Under old trees the shadow of young leaves
Dancing to please the wind along the grass,
Or the gold stillness of the August sun on the August sheaves;
Can I believe there is a heavenlier world than this?
And if there is
Will the heart of any everlasting thing
Bring me these dreams that take my breath away?
They come at evening with the home-flying rooks and the scent
of hay,
Over the fields. They come in spring.

## From a Window

Up here, with June, the sycamore throws
Across the window a whispering screen;
I shall miss the sycamore more I suppose,
Than anything else on this earth that is out in green.
But I mean to go through the door without fear,
Not caring much what happens here
When I'm away: -
How green the screen is across the panes
Or who goes laughing along the lanes
With my old lover all the summer day.

## Not for That City

Not for that city of the level sun,
    Its golden streets and glittering gates ablaze—
    The shadeless, sleepless city of white days,
White nights, or nights and days that are as one—
We weary, when all is said , all thought, all done.
    We strain our eyes beyond this dusk to see
    What, from the threshold of eternity
We shall step into. No, I think we shun
The splendour of that everlasting glare,
    The clamour of that never-ending song.
    And if for anything we greatly long,
It is for some remote and quiet stair
    Which winds to silence and a space for sleep
    Too sound for waking and for dreams too deep.

## Rooms

I remember rooms that have had their part
    In the steady slowing down of the heart.
The room in Paris, the room at Geneva,
The little damp room with the seaweed smell,
And that ceaseless maddening sound of the tide—
    Rooms where for good or for ill—things died.
But there is the room where we (two) lie dead,
Though every morning we seem to wake and might just as well seem to
    sleep again

As we shall somewhere in the other quieter, dustier bed

Out there in the sun—in the rain.

## Monsieur Qui Passe

  A purple blot against the dead white door

In my friend's rooms, bathed in their vile pink light,

I had not noticed her before

She snatched my eyes and threw them back to me:

She did not speak till we came out into the night,

Paused at this bench beside the kiosk on the quay.

God knows precisely what she said -

I left to her the twisted skein,

Though here and there I caught a thread, -

Something, at first, about "the lamps along the Seine,

And Paris, with that witching card of Spring

Kept up her sleeve, -why you could see

The trick done on these freezing winter nights!

While half the kisses of the Quay -

Youth, hope,-the whole enchanted string

Of dreams hung on the Seine's long line of lights."

Then suddenly she stripped, the very skin

Came off her soul,-a mere girl clings

Longer to some last rag, however thin,

When she has shown you-well-all sorts of things:
"If it were daylight-oh! one keeps one's head -
But fourteen years! -No one has ever guessed -
The whole thing starts when one gets to bed -
Death?-If the dead would tell us they had rest!
But your eyes held it as I stood there by the door -
One speaks to Christ-one tries to catch His garment's hem -
One hardly says as much to Him -no more:
It was not you, it was your eyes -I spoke to them."

She stopped like a shot bird that flutters still,
And drops, and tries to run again, and swerves.
The tale should end in some walled house upon a hill.
My eyes, at least, won't play such havoc there, -
Or hers -But she had hair! -blood dipped in gold;
And there she left me throwing back the first odd stare.
Some sort of beauty once, but turning yellow, getting old.
Pouah! These women and their nerves!
God! but the night is cold!


### Fin de Fête

Sweetheart, for such a day
One mustn't grudge the score;
Here, then, it's all to pay,
It's Good-night at the door.

Good-night and good dreams to you,-
Do you remember the picture-book thieves
Who left two children sleeping in a wood the long night through,
And how the birds came down and covered them with leaves?

So you and I should have slept, -But now,
Oh, what a lonely head!
With just the shadow of a waving bough
In the moonlight over your bed.

**I So Liked Spring**

I so liked Spring last year
Because you were here;-
The thrushes too-
Because it was these you so liked to hear-
I so liked you.

This year's a different thing,-
I'll not think of you.
But I'll like the Spring because it is simply spring
As the thrushes do.

## May, 1915

Let us remember Spring will come again
      To the scorched, blackened woods, where all the wounded trees
     Wait, with their old wise patience for the heavenly rain,
Sure of the sky: sure of the sea to send its healing breeze,
      Sure of the sun. And even as to these
      Surely the Spring, when God shall please
      Will come again like a divine surprise
To those who sit to-day with their great Dead, hands in their hands, eyes in their eyes,
At one with Love, at one with Grief: blind to the scattered things and changing skies.

## Old Shepherd's Prayer

Up to the bed by the window, where I be lyin',

Comes bells and bleat of the flock wi' they two children's clack.

Over, from under the eaves there's the starlings flyin',

And down in yard, fit to burst his chain, yapping out at Sue I do hear young Mac.

Turning around like a falled-over sack

I can see team plowin' in Whithy-bush field and meal carts startin' up road to Church-Town;

Saturday afternoon the men goin' back

And the women from market, trapin' home over the down.

Heavenly Master, I wud like to wake to they same green places

Where I be know'd for breakin' dogs and follerin' sheep.

And if I may not walk in th' old ways and look on th' old faces

I wud sooner sleep.


**On Youth Struck Down**
     (From an unfinished elegy)

Oh! Death what have you to say?
'Like a bride - like a bride-groom they ride away:
You shall go back to make up the fire,
To learn patience - to learn grief,
To learn sleep when the light has quite gone out of your earthly skies,
But they have the light in their eyes
     To the end of their day.'


**My Heart is Lame**

My heart is lame with running after yours so fast

Such a long way,

Shall we walk slowly home, looking at all the things we passed

Perhaps to-day?


Home down the quiet evening roads under the quiet skies,

Not saying much,

You for a moment giving me your eyes

When you could bear my touch.

But not to-morrow. This has taken all my breath;
Then, though you look the same,
There may be something lovelier in Love's face in death
As your heart sees it, running back the way we came;
  My heart is lame.


## The Call

From our low seat beside the fire
Where we have dozed and dreamed and watched the glow
Or raked the ashes, stopping so
We scarcely saw the sun or rain
Above, or looked much higher
Than this same quiet red or burned-out fire.
Tonight we heard a call,
A rattle on the window pane,
A voice on the sharp air,
And felt a breath stirring our hair,
A flame within us: Something swift and tall
Swept in and out and that was all.
Was it a bright or a dark angel? Who can know?
It left no mark upon the snow,
But suddenly it snapped the chain
Unbarred, flung wide the door
Which will not shut again;
And so we cannot sit here anymore.
We must arise and go:
The world is cold without
And dark and hedged about
With mystery and enmity and doubt,

But we must go
Though yet we do not know
Who called, or what marks we shall leave upon the snow.


## Absence

Sometimes I know the way

You walk, up over the bay;

It is a wind from that far sea

That blows the fragrance of your hair to me.


Or in this garden when the breeze

Touches my trees

To stir their dreaming shadows on the grass

I see you pass.


In sheltered beds, the heart of every rose

Serenely sleeps to-night. As shut as those

Your guarded heart; as safe as they form the beat, beat

Of hooves that tread dropped roses in the street.


Turn never again

On these eyes blind with a wild rain

Your eyes; they were stars to me. -

There are things stars may not see.


But call, call, and though Christ stands

Still with scarred hands

Over my mouth, I must answer. So
I will come -He shall let me go!

## The Trees are Down

> *—and he cried with a loud voice:*
> *Hurt not the earth, neither the sea, nor the trees—*
> *(REVELATION)*

They are cutting down the great plane-trees at the end of the gardens.
For days there has been the grate of the saw, the swish of the branches as they fall,
The crash of the trunks, the rustle of trodden leaves,
With the 'Whoops' and the 'Whoas,' the loud common talk, the loud common laughs of the men, above it all.

I remember one evening of a long past Spring
Turning in at a gate, getting out of a cart, and finding a large dead rat in the mud of the drive.
I remember thinking: alive or dead, a rat was a god-forsaken thing,
But at least, in May, that even a rat should be alive.

The week's work here is as good as done. There is just one bough
  On the roped bole, in the fine grey rain,
      Green and high
      And lonely against the sky.
        (Down now!—)
      And but for that,
      If an old dead rat
Did once, for a moment, unmake the Spring, I might never have thought
  of him again.

It is not for a moment the Spring is unmade to-day;
These were great trees, it was in them from root to stem:
When the men with the 'Whoops' and the 'Whoas' have carted the whole
  of the whispering loveliness away
Half the Spring, for me, will have gone with them.

It is going now, and my heart has been struck with the hearts of the
  planes;
Half my life it has beat with these, in the sun, in the rains,
      In the March wind, the May breeze,
In the great gales that came over to them across the roofs from the great
  seas.
      There was only a quiet rain when they were dying;
      They must have heard the sparrows flying,
And the small creeping creatures in the earth where they were lying—
      But I, all day, I heard an angel crying:
      'Hurt not the trees.'

## Smile, Death

Smile, Death, see I smile as I come to you

Straight from the road and the moor that I leave behind,

Nothing on earth to me was like this wind-blown space,

Nothing was like the road, but at the end there was a vision or a face

      And the eyes were not always kind.

  Smile, Death, as you fasten the blades to my feet for me,

On, on let us skate past the sleeping willows dusted with snow;

Fast, fast down the frozen stream, with the moor and the road and the vision behind,

  (Show me your face, why the eyes are kind!)

And we will not speak of life or believe in it or remember it as we go.

## To a Child in Death

You would have scoffed if we had told you yesterday
Love made us feel, or so it was with me, like some great bird
Trying to hold and shelter you in its strong wing: —
A gay little shadowy smile would have tossed us back such a solemn word,
And it was not for that you were listening When so quietly you slipped away
With half the music of the world unheard.

What shall we do with this strange summer, meant for you, —
Dear, if we see the winter through What shall be done with spring — ?
This, this is the victory of the grave; here is death's sting.
That it is not strong enough, our strongest wing.

But what of His who like a Father pitieth?
His Son was also, once, a little thing,
The wistfullest child that ever drew breath,
Chased by a sword from Bethlehem and in the busy house at Nazereth
Playing with little rows of nails, watching the carpenter's hammer swing,
Long years before His hands and feet were tied
And by a hammer and three great nails He died,
Of youth, of spring, Of sorrow, of loneliness, of victory the King,
Under the shadow of that wing.

# Moorland Night

My face is against the grass - the moorland grass is wet -
My eyes are shut against the grass, against my lips there are the little blades,
Over my head the curlews call, And now there is the night wind in my hair;
My heart is against the grass and the sweet earth, - it has gone still, at last;
It does not want to beat any more,
And why should it beat?
This is the end of the journey.
The Thing is found.

This is the end of all the roads -
Over the grass there is the night-dew
And the wind that drives up from the sea along the moorland road,
I hear a curlew start out from the heath
And fly off calling through the dusk,
The wild, long, rippling call -:
The Thing is found and I am quiet with the earth;
Perhaps the earth will hold it or the wind, or that bird's cry,
But it is not for long in any life I know. This cannot stay,
Not now, not yet, not in a dying world, with me, for very long;
I leave it here:
And one day the wet grass may give it back -

One day the quiet earth may give it back -

The calling birds may give it back as they go by -

To someone walking on the moor who starves for love and will not know

Who gave it to all these to give away;

Or, if I come and ask for it again

Oh! then, to me.

## At the Convent Gate

'Why do you shrink away, and start and stare?

Life frowns to see you leaning at death's gate

Not back, but on. Ah! sweet, it is too late:

You cannot cast these kisses from your hair.

Will God's cold breath blow kindly anywhere

Upon such burning gold? Oh! lips worn white

With waiting! Love will blossom in a night

And you shall wake to find the roses there!'


'Oh hush! He seems to stir, He lifts His Head.

He smiles. Look where He hangs against the sky.

He never smiled nor stirred, that God of pain

With tired eyes and limbs above my bed -

But loose me, this is death, I will not die -

Not while He smiles. Oh! Christ, Thine own again!'

# Requiescat

Your birds that call from tree to tree

Just overhead, and whirl and dart,

Your breeze fresh-blowing from the sea,

And your sea singing on, Sweetheart.


Your salt scent on the thin sharp air

Of this grey dawn's first drowsy hours,

While on the grass shines everywhere

The yellow sunlight of your flowers.


At the road's end your strip of blue

Beyond that line of naked trees-

Strange that we should remember you

As if you would remember these!


As if your spirit, swaying yet

To the old passions, were not free

Of Spring's wild magic, and the fret

Of the wilder wooing of the sea!

What threat of old imaginings,

Half-haunted joy, enchanted pain,

Or dread of unfamiliar things

Should ever trouble you again?

Yet you would wake and want, you said,

The little whirr of wings, the clear

Gay notes, the wind, the golden bed

Of the daffodil: and they are here!

Just overhead, they whirl and dart

Your birds that call from tree to tree,

Your sea is singing on - Sweetheart,

Your breeze is blowing from the sea.

Beyond the line of naked trees

At the road's end, your stretch of blue-

Strange if you should remember these

As we, ah! God! Remember you.

## The Little Portress

The stillness of the sunshine lies
Upon her spirit: silence seems
To look out from its place of dreams
When suddenly she lifts her eyes
To waken, for a little space,
The smile asleep upon her face.

A thousand years of sun and shower,
The melting of unnumbered snows
Go to the making of the rose
Which blushes out its little hour.
So old is Beauty: in its heart
The ages seem to meet and part.

Like Beauty's self, she holds a clear
Deep memory of hidden things -
The music of forgotten springs -
So far she travels back, so near
She seems to stand to patient truth
As old as Age, as young as Youth.

That is her window, by the gate.
Now and again her figure flits
Across the wall. Long hours she sits
Within: on all who come to wait.

Her Saviour too is hanging there
A foot or so above her chair.

'Soeur Marie de l'Enfant Jésus,'
You wrote it in my little book -
Your shadow-name. Your shadow-look
Is dimmer and diviner too,
But not to keep: it slips so far
Beyond us to that golden bar

Where angels, watching from their stair,
Half-envy you your tranquil days
Of prayer as exquisite as praise, -
Grey twilights softer than their glare
Of glory: all sweet human things
Which vanish with the whirr of wings.

Yet will you, when you wing your way
To whiter worlds, more whitely shine
Or shed a radiance more divine
Than here you shed from day to day -
High is His heaven a quiet star,
Be nearer God than now you are?

## Afternoon Tea

Please you, excuse me, good five-o'clock people,
   I've lost my last hatful of words,
And my heart's in the wood up above the church steeple,
   I'd rather have tea with - the birds.

Gay Kate's stolen kisses, poor Barnaby's scars,
   John's losses and Mary's gains,
Oh! what do they matter, my dears, to the stars
   Or the glow-worms in the lanes!

I'd rather lie under the tall elm-trees,
   With old rooks talking loud overhead,
To watch a red squirrel run over my knees,
   Very still on my brackeny bed.

And wonder what feathers the wrens will be taking
   For lining their nests next Spring;
Or why the tossed shadow of boughs in a great wind shaking
   Is such a lovely thing.

# Song

Oh! Sorrow, Sorrow, scarce I knew.
Your name when, shaking down the may
In sport, a little child, I grew
Afraid to find you at my play.
I heard it ere I looked at you;
You sang it softly as you came
Bringing your little boughs of yew
To fling across my gayest game.

Oh! Sorrow, Sorrow, was I fair
That when I decked me for a bride,
You met me stepping down the stair
And led me from my lover's side?
Was I so dear you could not spare
The maid to love, the child to play,
But coming always unaware,
Must bid and beckon me away?

Oh! Sorrow, Sorrow, is my bed
So wide and warm that you must lie
Upon it; toss your weary head
And stir my slumber with your sigh?
I left my love at your behest,
I waved your little boughs of yew,

But, Sorrow, Sorrow, let me rest,
For oh! I cannot sleep with you!

## An Ending

You know that road beside the sea,
Walled by the wavin' wheat
Which winds down to the litttle town
Wind-blown and grey and up the crooked street?
We'd used to meet
Just at the top, and when the grass was trodden down
'Twas by our feet
We'd used to stand
And watch the clouds like a great fleet
Sail over the sea and over the land,
And the gulls dart
Above our heads; and by the gate
At the road's end, when et was late
And all the ship's was showing lights on quiet nights,
We'd used to part.

So, Sir, you think I've missed my way,
There's nothing but the Judgement Seat -
But ef I pray perhaps I may - what's that you say -
A golden street?
Give me the yellow wheat!

Et edn't there we'm going to meet!
No, I'm not mazed, I make no doubt
That ef we don't my soul goes out
'Most like a candle in the everlasting dark.
And what's the odds? 'Twas just a spark
Alight for her.
I tell you, Sir,
That God He made et brave and plain,
Sin' he knows better than yon Book
What's in a look
You'd go to Hell to get again.

Another hour? An hour to wait - !
I sim I'll meet her at the gate -
You know that road beside the sea -
The crooked street - the wavin' wheat -?
(What's that? A lamp! Et made me start -)
That's where our feet - we'd used to meet - on quiet nights -
My God! the ships es showing lights! -
We'd used - to part.

**Left Behind**

Seventeen years ago you said
    Something that sounded like Good-bye;
        And everybody thinks that you are dead,
            But I.

    So I, as I grow stiff and cold
To this and that say Good-bye too;
        And everybody sees that I am old
            But you.

    And one fine morning in a sunny lane
Some boy and girl will meet and kiss and swear
        That nobody can love their way again
            While over there
You will have smiled, I shall have tossed your hair.


**A Farewell**

Remember me and smile, as smiling too,
    I have remembered things that went their way -
    The dolls with which I grew too wise to play -
Or over-wise -kissed, as children do,

And so dismissed them; yes, even as you

    Have done with this poor piece of painted clay -

    Not wantonly, but wisely, shall we say?

As one who, haply, tunes his heart anew.


Only I wish her eyes may not be blue,

    The eyes of a new angel. Ah! she may

Miss something that I found, -perhaps the clue

To those long silences of yours, which grew

    Into one word. And should she not be gay,

    Poor lady! Well, she too must have her day.

## To a Little Child in Death

Dear, if little feet make little journeys,
Thine should not be far;
Though beyond the faintest star,
Past earth's last bar,
Where angels are,
Thou hast to travel -
Cross the far blue spaces of the sea,
Climb above the tallest tree,
Higher up than many mountains be;

Sure there is some shorter way for thee,
Since little feet make little journeys.

Then, if smallest limbs are soonest weary,
Thou should'st soon be there;
Stumbling up the golden stair,
Where the angels' shining hair.
Brushes dust from baby faces.
Very, very gently cling
To a silver-edged wing,
And peep from under.
Then thou'lt see the King,
Then will many voices sing,
And thou wilt wonder.
Wait a little while
For Him to smile,
Who calleth thee.
He who calleth all,
Both great and small,
From over mountain, star and sea,
Doth call the smallest soonest to His knee,
Since smallest limbs are soonest weary.

**The Voice**

From our low seat beside the fire
Where we have dozed and dreamed, and watched the glow
Or raked the ashes, stooping so
We scarcely saw the sun and rain
Through the small curtained window-pane,
Or looked much higher
Than this same quiet red or burned-out fire,
Tonight we heard a call,
A voice on the sharp air,
And felt a breath stirring our hair,
A flame within us. Something swift and tall
Swept in and out and that was all.
Was it a bright or a dark angel? Who can know?
It made no mark upon the snow;
But suddenly, in passing, snapped the chain,
Unbarred, flung wide the door
Which will not shut again:
And so we cannot sit here any more.
We must arise and go.
The world is cold without
And dark and hedged about
With mystery and enmity and doubt,
But we must go,
Though yet we do not know
Who called, or what marks we shall leave upon the snow.

Printed in Great Britain
by Amazon